New Digital Media and Learning as an Emerging Area and "Worked Examples" as One Way Forward

D0721020

This book was made possible by grants from the John D. and Catherine T. MacArthur Foundation in connection with its grant making initiative on Digital Media and Learning. For more information on the initiative visit www.macfound.org.

The John D. and Catherine T. MacArthur Foundation Reports on Digital Media and Learning

The Future of Learning Institutions in a Digital Age by Cathy N. Davidson and David Theo Goldberg with the assistance of Zoë Marie Jones

New Digital Media and Learning as an Emerging Area and "Worked Examples" as One Way Forward by James Paul Gee

Living and Learning with New Media: Summary of Findings from the Digital Youth Project by Mizuko Ito, Heather Horst, Matteo Bittanti, danah boyd, Becky Herr-Stephenson, Patricia G. Lange, C. J. Pascoe, and Laura Robinson with Sonja Baumer, Rachel Cody, Dilan Mahendran, Katynka Z. Martínez, Dan Perkel, Christo Sims, and Lisa Tripp

Young People, Ethics, and the New Digital Media: A Synthesis from the Good-Play Project by Carrie James with Katie Davis, Andrea Flores, John M. Francis, Lindsay Pettingill, Margaret Rundle, and Howard Gardner

Confronting the Challenges of Participatory Culture: Media Education for the 21st Century by Henry Jenkins (P.I.) with Ravi Purushotma, Margaret Weigel, Katie Clinton, and Alice J. Robison

The Civic Potential of Video Games by Joseph Kahne, Ellen Middaugh, and Chris Evans

New Digital Media and Learning as an Emerging Area and "Worked Examples" as One Way Forward

James Paul Gee

The MIT Press
Cambridge, Massachusetts
London, England

For information about special quantity discounts, please email special _sales@mitpress.mit.edu.

This book was set in Stone Serif and Stone Sans by the MIT Press. Printed and bound in the United States of America.

Library of Congress Cataloging-in-Publication Data

Gee, James Paul.
New digital media and learning as an emerging area and "worked examples" as one way forward / James Paul Gee.
    p. cm.—(The John D. and Catherine T. MacArthur Foundation reports on digital media and learning)
Includes bibliographical references.
ISBN 978-0-262-51369-2 (pbk. : alk. paper)
1. Media literacy. 2. Digital media. 3. Mass media in education I. Title.
P96.M4.G34   2010   302.2'31071—dc22   2009023993

10 9 8 7 6 5 4 3 2

Contents

Series Foreword

The John D. and Catherine T. MacArthur Foundation Reports on Digital Media and Learning, published by the MIT Press, present findings from current research on how young people learn, play, socialize, and participate in civic life. The Reports result from research projects funded by the MacArthur Foundation as part of its $50 million initiative in digital media and learning. They are published openly online (as well as in print) in order to support broad dissemination and to stimulate further research in the field.

New Digital Media and Learning as an Emerging Area and "Worked Examples" as One Way Forward

Digital Media and Learning: An Emerging What?

Over the past few years, a new academic area has emerged around interest in digital media and learning (DMAL). Academics from a variety of different disciplines are contributing innovative research and interventions to this new endeavor (see, for example, the edited collections in the John D. and Catherine T. MacArthur Foundation Series on Digital Media and Learning: Bennett 2007; Buckingham 2007; Everett 2007; McPherson 2007; Metzger and Flanagin 2007; Salen 2007a). In this book, I consider how this new area might develop in the future and offer a specific proposal about how this development might be facilitated via what I call *worked examples*. I do this in light of how different areas of knowledge have developed and changed in the past, with a focus on areas now relevant to work on digital media and learning.

Before considering what might be the future of digital media and learning, I want to examine the different ways academic knowledge can be organized, beginning with the distinction between *field* and *discipline*. A field is a much less integrated configuration of academic work than a discipline. Areas like education and communications are fields, which are composed of multiple disciplines. However, over the years there has been a good deal of controversy in the field of education regarding whether it should stay a field or whether scholars should work to configure an integrated body of knowledge that would constitute education as a discipline. For whatever reason, no such integrated body of knowledge has emerged. On the other hand, an area like cognitive science has, over a number of decades, emerged as something like a discipline out of what were a disparate set of disciplines (e.g., computer science, mathematics, philosophy, linguistics, neuroscience, and psychology).

Discipline often has been defined in something like the following way: "An academic discipline, or field of study, is a branch of knowledge which is taught or researched at the college or university level" (http://en.wikipedia.org/wiki/Academic _discipline). However, disciplines as we name them in terms of university departments are not always fully coherent or even always cooperative units. Departments like biology and anthropology, for instance, house people from different and sometimes conflicting specializations or subdisciplines (e.g., in biology: molecular biology, developmental biology, genetics, environmental biology, marine biology; in anthropology: cultural anthropology, physical anthropology, archeology, linguistic anthropology). It is not uncommon, for instance, to have a biochemist or physical anthropologist look down on ecology or cultural anthropology as "less rigorous" science. Disciplines like biology, anthropology, and linguistics are historically and institutionally related constellations of different academic specializations.

I use the term *disciplinary specialization* (some people use *subdiscipline*) for academic specializations (like molecular biology or cultural anthropology) that are closer to the level of how academics engage in actual research. Such disciplinary specializations are areas of research and bodies of knowledge built around a narrow specialization with a shared set of rather narrowly defined questions, controversies, and methods.

Importantly, today, the nature of academic research is changing. It is common now, at the cutting edge of research, for researchers to work on a common theme using methods adapted from a variety of different disciplines and integrating different disciplinary perspectives and languages enough to work together. Work on complex adaptive systems would be a good example here (Lewin 1992; Waldrop 1992). Complex adaptive systems are complex systems that are composed of multiple interconnected elements and that are adaptive in the sense that they have the capacity to change and "learn" (adapt) from experience. Examples of such systems include the brain, immune systems, the stock market, ecological systems, cells, ant colonies, and some forms of social, institutional, and cultural organizations. John Holland and Murray Gell-Man at the Santa Fe Institute are among the pioneers who worked on such systems (Gell-Man 1994; Holland 1998). Scholars from a wide number of disciplines (e.g., computer science, history, physics, linguistics, biology, chemistry, and others) have contributed to this effort.

Work in the area of complex adaptive systems is not merely interdisciplinary. Scholars in the area are not just using different disciplines. They also share some substantive perspectives, tools, methods, and language and see some specific pieces of work in the area as exemplary for the area as a whole. For example, the principles of emergence and self-organization are crucial to anyone working in the area. More generally, methods and models used in the area are grounded in neo-Darwinian work on adaptation and evolution. This area of study is more integrated than a field like education; more is shared. However, the area is not yet a historically and institutionally established discipline, though it could become so in the future (and then there would be departments of complex adaptive systems and they would train graduate students under that label).

We need a name for these thematically defined areas. As there is no name for them as of yet in the literature, I call them *thematic disciplines*, because they are centered around a theme that cuts across many different disciplines and disciplinary specializations. Cognitive science, which I mentioned earlier, is an example of an area that some would consider a thematic discipline, although others believe that it has already become more akin to a traditional discipline (like biology or anthropology) because there are today some departments of cognitive science. This example indicates that we are working with a continuum here: field (e.g., education)—interdisciplinary work—thematic discipline (e.g., complex adaptive systems)—discipline (e.g., biology)—disciplinary specialization (e.g., genetics). Things on the left are broader and less tightly integrated than things on the right. In this book, when I want to avoid these terms, not distinguishing among them, I will simply use the term *(academic) area*, as I have been doing already. People often use the word *field* instead, but I already define that term more narrowly.

So, returning to new work on digital media and learning, what will come of such work? Right now, at best, digital media and learning is a loose configuration of scholars from different disciplinary specializations in different disciplines or fields. It is not yet even a field (using my definition). People working in the area come from the learning sciences, communication, media studies, educational technology, and many other places. The MacArthur Foundation and other funders have spent money on "field-building" projects. But will, or should, digital media and learning become a field like education or communication, a thematic discipline like the study of complex adaptive systems, a discipline like psychology, or a set of better-defined but loosely related disciplinary specializations in various different disciplines and fields?

We obviously cannot know at this point what will become of digital media and learning. But we can see that no real coherence in the area will occur if people in it do not achieve some degree of shared coherence and perspectives. So the question I ask in this book is: How can work in digital media achieve enough commonality for contributors to engage in fruitful collaboration and the accumulation of shared knowledge? If and when this happens, work in this area will become a field, a thematic discipline, or eventually a discipline of its own or a disciplinary specialization of some larger new discipline (e.g., digital culture) depending on how integration happens. In my view, the "deepest" thing that could happen to work in digital media and learning would be for it to become a thematic discipline. At the end of this book I offer a concrete proposal about one way we in DMAL could move the area forward to a more cohesive, integrated, and collaborative enterprise—namely, the production of what I call *worked examples* (using the term in a new way).

Although the question above is a key one in this book, before addressing it directly, I first consider what the emerging area of work on digital media and learning is—and how we, from different directions and disciplines, arrived at this shared interest that may or may not develop into something more. Before I start, though, let me point out that for anything to become a thematic discipline—to engage in the modern form of research in which different disciplines integrate around a big theme and some common tools and principles—there must exist a truly important and yet tractable theme around which the area can organize. Does digital media and learning have such a theme? One candidate would be this: the ways in which digital tools have transformed the human mind and human society and will do so further in the future. This certainly seems a big and important theme. The question, then, becomes whether there are shared tools and perspectives we all can develop to study it and whether it is tractable, that is, whether deep study will lead to real results.

We can learn something here from earlier work on literacy. Writing is a technology for making meaning, as are the various digital media, which is why we hear the term *digital literacies*. Literacy scholars from different disciplines (e.g., history, linguistics, anthropology, literary studies) pursued an analogous big theme to the one I stated earlier for digital media and learning: the ways in which literacy has transformed the human mind and human society (Havelock 1976; Goody 1977; Goody and

Watt 1963; Olson 1977; Ong 1982; Ong's classic 1982 book also started the discussion of the effects of digital media on traditional literacy and said it constituted a form of "secondary orality").

This theme never congealed into a coherent integrated body of scholarship. There were two reasons for this, in my view. First, scholars could not agree whether literacy, as a technology, transforms mind and society (i.e., has specific effects) or whether literacy has myriad different effects in different social, cultural, historical, and institutional contexts. In the latter case, the argument went, we should study the different contexts and not literacy in and of itself. We can, of course, expect the same conflict in the study of digital media. This dilemma did not foreclose a truly integrated approach to literacy, though it made it more difficult. Indeed, the "new literacy studies," which I discuss later, was an attempt to define something like a thematic discipline around literacy seen in contextually relevant terms.

Second, scholars studying literacy never came to share a core set of perspectives, principles, and tools. In my view, this partly resulted from the fact that the major literacy effect that interested policymakers and the wider society was, for better or worse, literacy learning in schools. And this concern was massively dominated by reading as a disciplinary specialization in psychology and reading education as a specialization in schools of education. People looked to these areas for implications and policy about learning and not to literacy studies as defined more generally. This, in turn, was closely tied to policymakers and the wider society largely viewing learning to read and write in purely mental and individual terms: Reading and writing go on in people's heads, and problems with them require remediation as a form of clinical therapy ("remedial reading therapy"). This viewpoint was challenged by the new literacy studies (as discussed later), but it meant that social, historical, institutional, and cultural aspects of literacy—the subject of much of work on literacy—took a decided backseat.

Digital media—themselves tools for meaning making, like writing—do not lend themselves strongly to a purely mental view in the way that reading and writing do (Gee 2004). There is something more apparently social and institutional about digital media. Thus, the area of digital media and learning may fare differently than did literacy. The argument for learning as larger than a purely mental and individual affair could be made much clearer, thereby tying scholarship and its societal and policy implications more tightly together than they were in the case of literacy research and literacy education. We should not forget that in a thematic discipline like the study of complex adaptive systems, a good deal of its power comes from the fact that scholarship in the area—much of which is indeed esoteric—has clear implications for society (e.g., on policymaking on the environment or on medical research). There is a caution here, then, for the emerging area of digital media and learning to develop strong ties to a wider view of learning both in terms of research and interventions. Digital media and learning cannot and should not, in my view, drop the strong tie to learning and become just *digital media studies* as a branch of cultural studies.

Where We Are and How We Got Here

Now I turn to the question of what the emerging area of work on digital media and learning is and how we, from different directions and disciplines, arrived at this shared interest. I consider, as well, the nature of several other emerged or emerging interdisciplinary areas of study, ones that are closely related to the concerns of the digital media and learning effort. One is the new literacy studies (NLS), an endeavor that proposed to study literacy (reading and writing) as a sociocultural achievement rather than a cognitive one. Another is situated cognition studies, a contemporary approach to mind and learning in the learning sciences that stresses the importance of experiences in the world to human thinking and problem solving and the ways in which these experiences are mediated by various tools and technologies. Yet another is the new literacies studies (not to be confused with new literacy studies, described above), an area that studies new "literacies"—new types of literacy beyond print literacy—especially new digital literacies and literacy practices embedded in contemporary popular culture. Finally, there is new media literacy studies, an area related to an older concern with media literacy regarding the ways in which people give meaning to and get meaning from various media.

I arrived at my own interest in digital media and learning via a route that led from the new literacy studies to an interest in video games and learning and thus to the new literacies studies. I realize this route is not typical and that others took other routes, starting from media studies, media literacy, communication, technology, education, the learning sciences, or other areas. We all have come from different places to this interest. But are we in the "same place" now? If so, what exactly is this place? How can we, coming from different disciplines and having taken different routes here, collaborate to define and develop this new place, our shared interest in digital media and learning?

After a few words here about video games, the place in which I have contributed to digital media and learning, I then lead on from there to what I see as some already-shared themes. After these introductory remarks, I discuss the emerged and emerging areas and then turn to a proposal about one way to achieve enough commonality for collaboration and the accumulation of knowledge to strengthen what has been, to date, a vibrant yet nascent area of research and intervention sitting at the intersection of digital media and learning.

In my book *What Video Games Have to Teach Us about Learning and Literacy* (Gee 2003; see also Gee 2004, 2005, 2007), I argue that good video games—which often are long, difficult, and complex—incorporate good learning principles for mastering the games. These principles, I argue, are also found in recent research in the learning sciences about how humans learn best

(Barab and Dede 2007; Barab and Roth 2006; Bransford, Brown, and Cocking 2000; diSessa 2000; Gee 2004; Hawkins 2005; Sawyer 2006; Wilensky and Reisman 2006).

Video-game designers did not become familiar with these learning principles from the learning sciences, nor did the learning sciences use video games as a basis for research. Rather, this is a matter of convergent development. Video games are largely just problem-solving spaces; if people could not learn them well and in an engaging fashion, the companies that make the games would go out of business. So it is, perhaps, not surprising that game designers have hit on—and even innovated on—many of the learning principles that contemporary research in the learning sciences has argued work for deep and effective human learning.

In my book, I argue that we should use these principles, with or without games, for learning inside and outside of school in areas that we value. The growing work on games and learning has led, however, to more and more interest in using not just the learning principles but video games themselves (both commercial entertainment games and "serious games") in schools and other learning sites (Shaffer 2004, 2005, 2007; Shaffer et al. 2005; Squire 2006, 2007; Squire and Jenkins 2004; Steinkuehler 2006, 2008a, 2008b).

Other people have come to the issue of new digital media and learning via other digital technologies than video games, such as social networking tools, media production tools, information tools like blogs and wikis, or a great many others. However, nearly everyone who has come to this issue has been impressed by the ways in which popular culture today is using digital tools and other devices to engage in powerful, deep, and complex thinking and learning outside of school (Gee 2004, 2007; Ito et al. 2010; Jenkins 2006a, 2006b; Johnson 2005). Popular culture itself thus has become a focus of the new work on digital media and learning.

For many young people, the digital and the nondigital fully intermix. Phenomena like Pokémon and Yu-Gi-Oh! are represented across a number of different media, including video games, card games played face to face, books, television shows, movies, and a plethora of Internet sites, including fan-fiction writing sites. Furthermore Pokémon and Yu-Gi-Oh! intermix in young people's popular culture with each other, with similar card games (e.g., Magic: The Gathering), and with the anime world more generally. In popular culture today, media and technologies (digital and nondigital) converge (Jenkins 2006a).

An equally impressive phenomenon has been the ways in which digital tools have allowed "everyday people" to produce and not just consume media. Today, they can use digital tools to create movies, games, music, newscasts, and many other things. And the products of these efforts can compete with professional work in appearance, and often in quality (Jenkins 2006a, 2006b).

Connected to this rise of production is a concomitant rise in participation (Black 2008; Jenkins 1992). There are two facets to this rise in participation. First, people do not have to serve just as spectators for the work of expert filmmakers, game designers, musicians, and news people; now they can participate readily in such activities thanks to this enhanced role of production (Jenkins 2006a, 2006b). More than half of all teenagers have created media content, and a third who use the Internet have shared content they produced (Lenhardt and Madden 2005). In many cases, these teens are actively involved in what Jenkins calls "participatory cultures" (Jenkins et al. 2009):

A participatory culture is a culture with relatively low barriers to artistic expression and civic engagement, strong support for creating and sharing creations, and some type of informal mentorship whereby experienced participants pass along knowledge to novices. (Jenkins et al. 2009, xi)

Second, with today's digital tools for social networking, people easily and readily can form and re-form groups to engage in joint activity (such as writing fan fiction) and even political interventions (such as campaigning) without the sanction and support of formal institutions. So participation today involves participating in both producer communities and in many other fluidly formed groups organized around a myriad of interests and passions (Shirky 2008).

Finally, a number of people working in the area of new digital media and learning have pointed out how today's popular cultural activities often involve quite complex language, thinking, and problem solving (Gee 2004, 2007; Johnson 2005). The plot of a TV show like *Wired*—with its many subplots and complex relationships among its characters—is so complex that old-fashioned TV shows pale by comparison. The language on a Yu-Gi-Oh! card or Web site is more complex, technical, and specialist than many young people see in school. The thinking, problem solving, and collaboration skills required to engage in video game "modding" (modification) look more like important twenty-first-century skills than do the skills on offer in some of our skill-and-drill-test prep schools. So do the social, technical, and organizational skills required to lead a guild in World of Warcraft. It even appears that the reasoning required to engage in debates on many Internet forums involving technical matters (e.g., making mods for Warcraft) often resembles valued forms of scientific reasoning, forms that we have difficulty gaining in school with all our textbooks (Steinkuehler 2006, 2008a, 2008b).

We live, then, in an age of convergent media, production, participation, fluid group formation, and cognitive, social, and linguistic complexity—all embedded in contemporary popular culture. Digital tools help create and sustain these features of "modern times," but they do not stand alone and cannot be studied in isolation from these features.

All this leads me to a value-laden statement about what I see as one fundamental principle that, in my view, has begun to unite some work on digital media and learning: The emerging area of digital media and learning is not just the study of how digital tools can enhance learning. It is, rather, the study of how digital tools and new forms of convergent media, production, and participation, as well as powerful forms of social organization and complexity in popular culture, can teach us how to enhance learning in and out of school and how to transform society and the global world as well.

In many respects, the contemporary interest in digital media and learning needs a better name or label because we are concerned with more than just new technologies in any narrow sense. A new label would have to incorporate the themes of convergent media, production, participation, fluid group formation, complexity, and popular culture. I do not here offer a new name, precisely because I want to problematize what it means to talk about digital media and learning as an emerging area or to talk about emergent academic areas at all. Digital media and learning as an emerging area of study is related to, in complex ways, a number of other emerged or emerging areas. So right now it is not important to properly name what I have been calling *digital media and learning* as an area of convergent interest. I simply abbreviate it as *DMAL* while we wait for a proper name.

In this book, I discuss DMAL as an emerging area and consider its potential core contributors or members only as people who want to study digital media and learning in the larger context that I tried briefly to delimit earlier (convergent media, production, participation, complexity, and popular culture). Such people probably all would name their interest differently.

The core issue is this: Do people who recognize my discussion of DMAL—whatever they personally call their interest—have enough in common to serve as the foundation for collaboration and the joint accumulation of knowledge? How can such a common foundation be built to underwrite collaboration, accumulation of knowledge, and a coherent area, whether this turns out to be a field, discipline, or thematic discipline?

The New Literacy Studies

Now I take up the question of how we arrived at an interest in DMAL. I talk about how I got here, because one of my points is that different people got here in different ways and eventually we need to recognize and learn from these different paths. The different routes people took on their way to an interest in digital media and learning are a great strength because of the diversity of ideas and methods they bring with them to the research and practice. But this diversity also can make issues of commonality, collaboration, and the joint accumulation of shared knowledge problematic. At the same time, the different paths taken are beginning to influence others in this emerging area through our interaction with each other.

I start this examination with an area that was "emerging" many years ago, an area that has both influenced DMAL and suggests implications for how DMAL can develop as an area. In my book *Sociolinguistics and Literacies* (Gee 1990) I attempt to name what I then saw as an emerging new area of study. I called this area the *new literacy studies*; today it is sometimes just referred to as the *NLS* (Brandt and Clinton 2002; Gee 2000; Hull and Schultz 2001; Pahl and Rowsel 2005, 2006; Prinsloo and Mignonne 1996; Street 1993, 1995, 1997, 2005).

The NLS was composed of scholars from linguistics, history, anthropology, rhetoric and composition studies, cultural psychology, education, and other areas (e.g., Bazerman 1989; Cazden 1988; Cook-Gumperz 1986; Gee 1987; Graff 1979; Heath 1983; Scollon and Scollon 1981; Scribner and Cole 1981; Street 1984; Wertsch 1985). These people certainly saw themselves as related in some sense and, for the most part, they knew each other. But they did not then, nor later, necessarily agree on what—if anything—made them part of one emerging area. Other people, however, did begin to see them as part of something new beyond their specific disciplines.

The NLS opposed a traditional psychological approach to literacy. Such an approach viewed literacy as a "cognitive phenomenon" and defined it in terms of mental states and mental processing. The "ability to read" and "the ability to write" were treated as things people did inside their heads. The NLS instead saw literacy as something people did inside society. It argued that literacy was not primarily a mental phenomenon, but rather a sociocultural one. Literacy was a social and cultural achievement—it was about ways of participating in social and cultural groups—not just a mental achievement. Thus, literacy needed to be understood and studied in its full range of contexts—not just cognitive but social, cultural, historical, and institutional, as well.

Traditional psychology saw readers and writers as engaged in mental processes like decoding, retrieving information, comprehension, inferencing, and so forth. The NLS saw readers and writers as engaged in social or cultural *practices*. Written language is used differently in different practices by different social and cultural groups. And, in these practices, written language never sits all by itself, cut off from oral language and action. Rather, within different practices, it is integrated with different ways of using oral language; different ways of acting and interacting; different ways of knowing, valuing, and believing; and, too, often different ways of using various sorts of tools and technologies.

For example, people read and write religious texts differently from legal ones and differently again from biology texts or texts in popular culture, such as fan fiction or strategy guides for video games. Also, people can read the same text in different ways for different purposes. For example, they can read the Bible as theology, as literature, as history, or as a self-help guide. They can read a comic book as entertainment, as insider details for expert fans, as cultural critique, or as heroic mythology. People also do things with these texts that often involve more than just reading and writing, and they do them with other people—people like fundamentalists, lawyers, biologists, manga otaku, gamers, or whatever—who sometimes (often) make judgments about who are "insiders" and who are not. Lawyers practice law, chemists do chemistry, fans engage in fandom, gamers game. These are all activities in which texts are put to multiple uses; for example, as evidence in a court trial, as techniques to follow in chemistry experiments, as social bonding mechanisms for fans, and as strategy guides to help a gamer out of tight spot in a game. Knowing how to use a text in the right place and time is as important as knowing how to "decode" it.

So, what determines how one reads or writes in a given case? Not just what is in one's head, but also the conventions, norms, values, and practices of different social and cultural groups: lawyers, gamers, historians, religious groups, and schools, for instance, or larger cultural groups like (certain types of) Native Americans, African Americans, or "middle class" people. For example, Ron and Suzanne Scollon (1981) argue that some Native American and Canadian groups view essays (a prototypical literacy form in school) quite differently than do many Anglo-Americans and Canadians. Athabaskians—the group the Scollons studied in the United States and Canada—have a cultural norm in which they prefer to communicate only in known circumstances with people who are already known.

Essays require the writer to communicate to a "fictional" audience—the assumed general "rational reader," not someone already known—and, thus, violate a cultural communicational norm for Athabaskians. To write an essay, for Athabaskians, is to engage in a form of cross-cultural conflict. Essays are not "neutral" but socially, historically, and culturally value-laden; indeed, how, when, and why they arose in history is a well-studied phenomenon.

People learn a given way of reading or writing by participating in (or at least coming to understand) the distinctive social and cultural practices of different groups. When these groups teach or "apprentice" people to read and write in certain ways, they never stop there. They teach them to act, interact, talk, know, believe, and value in certain ways as well, ways that "go with" how they write and read (Gee 1990). So, for example, knowing how to read or write a game faq (a strategy guide for a video game) requires knowing how game faqs are used in the social practices of gamers, practices that involve much more than just reading and writing. It requires knowing how gamers talk about, debate over, and act in regard to such things as "spoilers" and "cheats"—and how "cheating" is defined by gamers, not just in general terms (Consalvo 2007).

The same is true of knowing how to write or read a legal document, a piece of literary criticism, a religious tract, or a memo from the boss. One can develop an appreciation for some texts without participating in the practices of the group whose texts they are, but a knowledge of how the "texts" fit into those practices is still necessary. And being a "central participant" requires prior participation and "apprenticeship" with the group (Lave 1996; Lave and Wenger 1991). Many different social and cultural practices incorporate literacy, so, too, there many different "literacies" (legal literacy, gamer literacy, country music literacy, academic literacy of many different types). People do not just read and write in general, they read and write specific sorts of "texts" in specific ways; these ways are determined by the values and practices of different social and cultural groups.

These multiple literacies are why the NLS often tended to study not literacy itself directly, but such things as "activity systems" (Engeström 1987), "Big D Discourses" (Gee 1990), "discourse communities" (Bizzell 1992), "cultures" (Street 1995), "communities of practices" (Lave and Wenger 1991; Wenger 1998), "actor-actant networks" (Latour 2005), "collectives" (Latour 2004), or "affinity groups" or "affinity spaces" (Gee 2004)—the names differ and there are others, but they are all names for ways in which people socioculturally organize themselves to engage in activities. The morale was: follow the social, cultural, institutional, and historical organizations of people (whatever one calls them) first and then see how literacy is taken up and used in those organizations, along with action, interaction, values, and tools and technologies.

As I mention at the outset of this book, long before the NLS came on the scene, already there had been a good deal of work—stemming from different disciplines—on literacy in its historical, cultural, and institutional contexts. What differentiated the NLS from this work—some of which it attacked—was the issue of whether literacy in and of itself as a technology has specific cognitive and societal effects. Some influential scholars had argued that literacy reshaped the human mind and transformed society, making people more intelligent, more humane, and more modern (e.g., Havelock 1976; Olson 1977; Ong 1982). The NLS disputed this claim (e.g., Street 1984) and, in turn, claimed that literacy had very different effects in different contexts of use—some good and some not—and no inherent effects across all contexts (Gee 1990, 1992). Unfortunately, in this debate neither side talked about the "affordances" of literacy—that is, the effects it tends to have, all things being equal, in different contexts, if these effects are not otherwise mitigated. Such an approach might have yielded more compromise and collaboration. And, indeed, I advocate such an approach when we are talking about digital media as technologies.

The NLS—thanks to its opposition to traditional cognitive psychology (not to mention its hostility to earlier forms of psychology like behaviorism) tended to have little or nothing to say about the mind or cognition. It paid attention only to the social, cultural, historical, and institutional contexts of literacy. It had little to say about the individual apart from the individual's "membership" in various social and cultural groups. Thus, it also had little to say about learning as an individual phenomenon. Learning was largely treated—if it was treated at all—as changing patterns of participation in "communities of practice" (Lave and Wenger 1991).

In my view, the NLS never fully cohered as an area. Although there are now books devoted to it as a unitary phenomenon, there was never any attempt to translate across the diverse disciplinary languages within which different contributors wrote. We each had our allegiances to different academic microcommunities with our own pattern of citations, for instance. Was this a serious problem? In my view it was; perhaps others would not agree. I believe the NLS made less progress—beyond its initial successes—than it might otherwise have done. The issue is obviously germane to the fate of DMAL.

The NLS argued that print literacy is a technology for giving and getting meaning that has no single effect but many different ones in different social, institutional, cultural, and historical contexts. The same is true for for digital literacy, with the caution I mentioned above that we should pay attention to the affordances of different technologies. It is also a technology (made up of many different kinds of tools and associated practices) for giving and getting meaning. These tools, too, have no single effect (good or bad) but many different ones in different social, institutional, cultural, and historical contexts. Just as the NLS wanted to study literacy in terms of larger social organizations, DMAL wants to study digital media in terms of larger social and learning organizations built around them. I point out later how the NLS—and the other areas I survey in this book— have influenced people in DMAL even if they have not read most of the literature in these areas.

Situated Cognition

I pointed out previously that the NLS talked little about learning at the level of the individual, largely due to its hostility to psychology. However, in the 1980s psychology itself began to change. New movements in "cognitive science" and the "learning sciences" began to argue that the mind is furnished primarily not by abstract concepts but by records of actual experience (e.g., Barsalou 1999a, 1999b; Churchland and Sejnowski 1992; Clark 1989, 1993, 1997; Damasio 1994; Gee 1992; Glenberg 1997; Kolodner 1993, 2006).

Previous work in cognitive psychology—often based on the idea that the human mind is like a digital computer—argued that memory is severely limited, as it is in a digital computer (Newell and Simon 1972). This newer work argued that human memory is nearly limitless and that we can and do store almost all our actual experiences in our heads and use these experiences to reason about similar experiences or new ones in the future (Gee 2004; Churchland 1986; Churchland 1989; Churchland and Sejnowski 1992).

This newer work came in many different varieties and constituted a "family" of related but not identical viewpoints. For
want of a better name, we might call the family *situated cognition studies* (see also Brown, Collins, and Dugid 1989; Hawkins
2005; Hutchins 1995; Lave and Wenger 1991). These viewpoints
all believe that thinking is connected to, and changes across,
actual situations and is not usually a process of applying abstract
generalizations, definitions, or rules.

Situated cognition studies argues that thinking is tied to experiences of goal-oriented action in the material and social world.
Furthermore, these experiences are stored in the mind/brain not
in terms of abstract concepts but in something like dynamic
images tied to perception of the world and of our own bodies,
internal states, and feelings (Churchland 1986; Damasio 1994;
Gee 1992). Thus, consider the following quotes, which give the
flavor of what it means to say that cognition is situated in
embodied experience:

- "Comprehension is grounded in perceptual simulations that
prepare agents for situated action." (Barsalou 1999a, 77)
- "To a particular person, the meaning of an object, event, or
sentence is what that person can do with the object, event, or
sentence." (Glenberg 1997, 3)
- "Increasing evidence suggests that perceptual simulation is
indeed central to comprehension." (Barsalou 1999a, 74)
- "Higher intelligence is not a different kind of process from
perceptual intelligence." (Hawkins 2005, 96)

Human understanding, then, is not primarily a matter of stor-
ing general concepts in the head or applying abstract rules to

experience. Rather, humans think, understand, and learn best when they use their prior experiences (so they must have had some) as a guide to prepare themselves for action. I talk later about how they do this.

Work on situated cognition goes beyond the digital computer as a model of the human mind. Rather, it often uses as a model so-called *connectionist* or *parallel distributed computers* (i.e., *networked*) (Churchland 1986; Churchland 1989; Churchland and Sejnowski 1992; Gee 1992; Rumelhart, McClelland, and the PDP Research Group 1986). Connectionist computers look for and store patterns (networks of associations) among elements of input from the world. The argument is that humans—like connectionist computers—look for patterns in the elements of their experiences in the world and, as they have more and more experiences, find deeper and more subtle patterns, which help predict what might happen in the future when they act to accomplish goals.

For example, say I ask you to think of a typical bedroom (Gee 1992; Rumelhart, McClelland, and the PDP Research Group 1986). Thanks to your experiences in the world, what you think of may be a room of moderate size with things like a bed, side tables, a dresser, drapes, lamps, pictures, a clock, a carpet, and other things. These things have all been elements in your experiences with rooms, elements that you have come to see as a pattern (or network of elements). But, say, I tell you there is a small refrigerator in the bedroom. Now you may envision a student's bedroom in a dorm (e.g., a smaller room, a bed, a desk, a lamp on the desk, and maybe a mess on the floor). You have formed a different pattern out of the elements of your experience. This example shows how you use elements of your actual experience to think, not a static schema or rule system. Such associations (about bedrooms or anything else), and how you use them, change as you gain different experiences. For example, with new experiences, the idea of bedroom with a refrigerator may end up triggering an image of a poverty-level hotel room. You can see the same thing happening with "The coffee spilled; go get a mop" (where you bring in an association with coffee as a liquid) versus "The coffee spilled, go get a broom" (where you bring in an association with coffee as grains). Compare also "The coffee spilled, stack it again" (Clark 1993).

Despite the NLS having lacked interest in the mind, there is a natural affinity between situated cognition studies and the NLS. This affinity has, for the most part, not been much built on from either side. Situated cognition studies argues that we think through paying attention to elements of our experiences. Although this is a claim about the mind, we can ask what determines which experiences a person has and how they pay attention to those experiences (i.e., how they find patterns in their experiences or to which patterns they pay attention).

One answer to this question is that participation in the practices of various social and cultural groups determines which experiences a person has and how they pay attention to the elements of these experiences. Related to our interests in DMAL, these practices are mediated by various tools and technologies whether these be print or digital media or other tools. Of course, that was just what the NLS wanted to study. For example, bird watching clubs and expert bird watchers shape how new bird watchers pay attention to their experience of birds and environments in the field (Gee 1992). And these experiences are mediated in important ways by various tools and technologies (e.g., bird books, scopes, and binoculars). Obviously a bird watcher experiences a wood duck in a vastly different way when looking at it through a powerful scope than through unaided vision. Furthermore, such technologies allow distinctive social practices to arise that could not exist otherwise (e.g., debating the details of tiny aspects of feathers on hard-to-distinguish gulls).

Thus, a situated view of the mind leads us to social and cultural groups and their tools and technologies. Both situated cognition studies and the NLS point not to the "private mind" but to the world of experience—and that experience is almost always shared in social and cultural groups—as the core of human learning, thinking, problem solving, and literacy (where *literacy* is defined as "getting and giving meanings using written language"). This was the argument I made in my book *The Social Mind* (Gee 1992) at a time when I was trying to integrate learning into the NLS and to link situated cognition studies and the NLS.

Situated cognition studies has cohered as an area, largely as a result of the shared background of most of its adherents in contemporary psychology. However, as situated cognition studies has become an integral part of the learning sciences, a discipline often found in educational psychology departments, it has begun to face more variety of backgrounds from people entering the discipline trained in areas outside psychology, such as media studies or ethnography (Sawyer 2006).

Situated cognition studies and the contemporary learning sciences, of which it is a part, are the basis of the learning theories that inform much work in DMAL—sometimes overtly when this work is done by learning scientists, and sometimes covertly by those from other areas who have picked up the influences indirectly through interaction with those learning scientists. This is not to say that the learning theories behind various pieces of work in DMAL are identical (c.f. Barab and Roth 2006, and Gee 1992, 2004). There are, indeed, variations in the midst of commonalities, but there is not space, nor need, here to discuss these variations. Nonetheless, situated cognition studies, in some guise, is liable to remain the crucial learning theory behind DMAL as (or if) it develops into an ever-more-integrated and coherent area of studies.

Let me append a note here relevant to DMAL. Work on situated cognition stresses that knowledge and intelligence are contextual, embodied, and distributed (across various tools and technologies, as well as across groups of people). There are, however, forms of cognitive psychology today that gives little attention to those aspects of knowledge and intelligence and instead still stress mental representations and mental processing (e.g., Kirschner, Sweller, and Clark 2006). These latter forms of cognitive psychology tend to underpin a good deal of work in instructional technology, including work on games and simulations. Such work tends to stress breaking learning down into its smallest bits and sequencing these bits; in contrast, work inspired by situated cognition tends to stress learning in terms of whole practices in actual contexts with collaboration and various tools and technologies. This has given rise to quite different approaches and is an apparent divide in work in DMAL. It is clear which side I take and, without doubt, this influences my approach in this book. I do think there may be some compromise to made here—and, indeed, there is a good discussion to be had about whether certain types of learning tasks better fit one paradigm than another. But discussing this divide, which deserves its own examination, is beyond the scope of this book.

The New Literacies Studies

The NLS argued that written language is a technology for giving and getting meaning. In turn, what written language means is a matter determined by the social, cultural, historical, and institutional practices of different groups of people. The new litera*cies* studies simply carries over the NLS argument about written language to new digital technologies. The *new literacies studies* is parsed grammatically differently than the *new literacy studies*. The NLS was about studying literacy in a new way. The new literacies studies is about studying new types of literacy beyond print literacy, especially digital literacies and literacy practices embedded in popular culture. I am aware this is confusing, but the naming issue emerged partly because people in the new literacies studies were influenced by—and, in part, responding to or supplementing—the NLS.

The new literacies studies views different digital tools as technologies for giving and getting meaning, just like language (Coiro et al. 2008; Gee 2004, 2007; Kist 2004; Kress 2003; Knobel and Lankshear 2007; Lankshear 1997; Lankshear and Knobel 2006). Like the NLS, the new literacies studies also argues that the meanings to which these technologies give rise are determined by the social, cultural, historical, and institutional practices of different groups of people. And, as with the NLS, these practices almost always involve more than just using a digital tool; they involve, as well, ways of acting, interacting, valuing, believing, and knowing, in addition to often using other sorts of tools and technologies, including oral and written language.

Just as the NLS wanted to talk about different literacies in the plural—that is, different ways of using written language within different sorts of sociocultural practices—so, too, the new literacies studies wants to talk about different digital literacies—that is, different ways of using digital tools within different sorts of sociocultural practices. In this sense, the new literacies studies is a natural offshoot of the NLS, though the two areas do not contain the same people by any means.

The new literacies studies has an important historical relationship with the NLS, from which it partly stems. At the same time as the new literacies studies has been emerging as an area of study, another area has emerged: the *new media literacy studies* (*NMLS* for short). The NMLS has not had a significant historical relationship with the NLS, at least until recently (thanks to different people now meeting each other as they come to DMAL from different places), nor does it in any significant way stem from the NLS. In many ways DMAL is an amalgam of the new literacies studies with media literacy and contemporary learning theory (as in situated cognition studies). Each area, though, has influenced different people in DMAL differently, and people have brought to the area yet other influences (e.g., game design).

New Media Literacy Studies

The NMLS is an offshoot of a movement that has been around for some time: media literacy (on NMLS and its relation to traditional media literacy, see, e.g., Beach 2006; Brunner and Tally 1999; Buckingham 2003, 2007; Hobbs 1997, 2007; Jenkins et al. 2009; Warschauer 1998). Both the NMLS and the earlier media literacy are connected in large part to people in the field of communications or related fields, though interest in both has spread well beyond communications.

Media literacy as an area was concerned with how people give meaning to and get meaning from media, that is, things like advertisements, newspapers, television, and film. Of course, the process sometimes involves giving and getting meaning from oral and written language—language used in media contexts—and from images, sounds, and "multimodal texts" (texts that mix images and/or sounds with words) as well.

Media literacy scholars did not want to study just how people give meaning to and get meaning from media; they also wanted to intervene in such matters by studying how people can be made more "critical" or "reflective" about the sorts of meanings they give to and get from media. People can be "manipulated" by media and can "manipulate" others with media. It is often relevant to ask whose (vested) interest is served by a given media message and to wonder whether people often mistake whose interest such messages really serve. For example, an ad's message really serves the profit motives of a company but can (mistakenly) appear to a consumer to be in his or her best interest. Such an approach also raised issues about the extent to which consumers of media are "dupes" or "savvy." Some approaches to media literacy tended to stress the ways in which consumers could and sometimes do use media and media messages for their own interests and desires, even in ways that the producers of those messages did not intend (Alvermann, Moon, and Hagood 1999; Lankshear and Knobel 2006). The extent to which such proactive use of media is or is not a politically effective counter to consumerism and the power of profit-seeking businesses is a matter of debate.

The NMLS inherited a good deal of the concerns and issues of media literacy. However, today it is not just media professionals and corporations that can produce and manipulate people with media. Everyday people—former consumers—now can produce their own media and compete with professionals and corporations. Thus, the NMLS stresses the ways in which digital tools and the media built from them are transforming society and, in particular, popular culture. At the outset of this book, I discuss some of the transformations to which digital tools are giving rise, in terms of production and not just consumption and participation and not just spectatorship.

These transformations are crucial to the NMLS. Digital tools are changing the balance of production and consumption in media. It is easier today for everyday people—not just experts and elites—not just to consume media but also to produce it themselves. This includes producing professional-looking movies, newscasts, video games (through "modding"), and many other products. This production means that digital tools are changing the balance of participation and spectatorship. More and more, people do not have to play just the role of the spectator because they now can produce their own music, news, games, and films, for example; these practices once were reserved for professional or elite musicians, filmmakers, game designers, and journalists.

Furthermore, digital tools are changing the nature of groups, social formations, and power. Prior to our current digital tools, it was hard to start and sustain a group. It usually required an institution, with all its attendant bureaucracy and top-down power. Today, with Web sites like Flicker, MySpace, and Facebook, and digital devices like mobile phones, it is easier than ever to form and join groups, even for quite short-term purposes. Often no formal institution is required and groups can organize themselves bottom-up through constant communication and feedback. These quickly formed groups can engage in social, cultural, and political action in a fast, pervasive, and efficient manner. Such groups can readily form and re-form, transforming themselves as circumstances change. In fact, it can sometimes be hard for more traditional groups and institutions to keep up with such flexible group formation.

All the above trends are leading to the phenomenon known as *pro-ams*. Today young people are using the Internet and other digital tools outside of school to learn and even become experts in a variety of domains. We live in the age of pro-ams: amateurs who have become experts at whatever they have developed a passion for (Anderson 2006; Gee 2008; Leadbeater and Miller 2004). Many of these are young people who use the Internet, communication media, digital tools, and membership in often virtual, but sometimes real, communities of practice to develop technical expertise in a plethora of different areas. Some of these areas are digital video, video games, digital storytelling, machinima, fan fiction, history and civilization simulations, music, graphic art, political commentary, robotics, anime, fashion design (e.g., for Sims characters). In fact, there are now pro-ams in nearly every endeavor the human mind envision.

These pro-ams have passion and go deep rather than wide. At the same time, pro-ams are often adept at pooling their skills and knowledge with other pro-ams to bring off bigger tasks or to solve larger problems. These are people who do not necessarily know what everyone else knows, but do know how to collaborate with other pro-ams to put knowledge to work to fulfill their intellectual and social passions.

The NMLS thus engages with a new sense of *media literacy*. The emphasis is not just on how people respond to media messages, but also on how they engage proactively in a media world where production, participation, social group formation, and high levels of nonprofessional expertise are prevalent. Issues of being critical and reflective are still paramount, of course, but so are issues of how digital media are and are not changing the balance of power and status in society.

Influence

My summary of emerged and emerging areas relevant to DMAL traces only one trajectory to DMAL. Other trajectories would tell the story in different ways. As people from different backgrounds have come to DMAL, they have influenced each other through personal interactions. These interactions have caused elements of the NLS, the new literacies studies, situated cognition studies, and NMLS to circulate even apart from the formal literature.

For example, consider two important papers by Katie Salen (2007b) and Eric Zimmerman (2007), the authors together of a very influential book on game design (Salen and Zimmerman 2003). Both these illuminating papers deal with video gaming as a literacy. They both argue, among other things, that the sorts of meanings gamers give to and get from playing and modding involve "systems thinking" and "design thinking" within communities of practice that encourage technologically mediated, collaborative problem-solving. Such thinking and collaboration are, they argue, particularly important twenty-first-century skills. These authors, both innovative game designers, were influenced as much by contact with people from the movements I discuss here—people who had moved to DMAL—as they were by the formal literature in these areas. For example, both Salen and Zimmerman attended a series of Spencer Foundation–sponsored meetings (2005–2007) that brought together people from the NLS, the new literacies studies, the NMLS, and situated cognition studies with game scholars and game designers (for a report on these meetings, see Gee 2007, chapter 10). Both Salen and Zimmerman injected into those meeting their own unique approach to game design. In turn, they meld all these interests in their 2007 papers.

Further, both Katie Salen (2007b) and Henry Jenkins—the leading NMLS scholar in the world today—in his important 2006 white paper (later published as a book, Jenkins et al. 2009) cite the work of the New London Group (1996). The New London Group was a small international group of scholars (of which I was a member) that wrote a manifesto on literacy for "new times." The manifesto gave rise to the term *multiliteracies,* which was something of an amalgam of the NLS, the new literacies studies, and situated cognition studies (and other movements), stressing print literacy as multiple sociocultural practices, new digital literacies, and multimodality (the mixing and integration of print, images, and other modalities) all in terms of our quickly changing global world.

Thus, the emerged and emerging areas I have discussed are relevant both as formal literature and as influences "in the air" as people from different backgrounds meet, interact, and influence each other. If DMAL ever does emerge as an integrated area, these sorts of personal interactions will be as much a part of its history as the formal literature. In fact, the way forward to more commonality, sharing, collaboration, and accumulated knowledge is not through more reading and citing of formal literature; rather, it is through being more overt with each other in DMAL about our assumptions, influences, and approaches. I address this matter in the next chapter.

Worked Examples: A Proposal about How to Move Forward

In *Sociolinguistics and Literacies* (Gee 1990), I attempted to show something unitary in a body of diverse work and called it the *new literacy studies* (NLS). I did this by singling out specific cases of what I took to be and argued to be prototypical work in the area. I compared and juxtaposed these prototypical cases, hoping that people would then see them as examples of "one thing," the NLS.

The prototypical cases I used were Shirley Brice Heath's (1983) work on class and racial differences in how families read books to their children; Sylvia Scribner and Michael Cole's (1981) work on literacy practices in Liberia in Africa; Brian Street's (1984) work on literacy practices in Iran; Ron and Suzanne Scollon's (1981) work (mentioned earlier) on Athabaskan views of school-based literacy compared to those of Anglo-Americans and Anglo-Canadians; Harvey Graff's (1979) work on the history of literacy; and work that people like Sarah Michaels (1981), Courtney Cazden (1985), and I (Gee 1985) had done on the differences between black and white children's talk at "sharing time" in early schooling.

What I did not do—could not do at the time—was get each of these people to explicate how and why they had carried out their work in the way in which they had and how this compared and contrasted with the other cases I had taken as prototypical, cases coming from different disciplinary backgrounds. I did not get the authors to comment on how they viewed the other pieces of work I had singled out or to say how they would have engaged with such work from their own perspective. In fact, in academics there really are no mechanisms for this type of cross-disciplinary dialog. Journals and other scholarly practices mostly ensure that no such dialog happens and that we respond, at best, to people who share our discipline or even just our disciplinary specialty. As the NLS developed, a little of this dialog did happen, though only sporadically.

Of course, I did try in *Sociolinguistics and Literacies* to compare and contrast the different prototypical cases, but what was really needed—and is, in fact, rare in academics—is for different authors to explicate the foundations of their work in ways that compare and contrast these foundations with the foundations for other people's related work. Such foundations almost always are taken for granted as part of the disciplinary background of people's research; rarely are they directly confronted in comparison to other people's different disciplinary foundations. Although within a discipline (usually within a disciplinary specialty)—anthropology (e.g., cultural anthropology), for instance—people will compare and contrast different approaches in the discipline (usually a new one against an old or traditional one), people do this much less commonly across disciplines. So, for instance, although it was clear to me that the Scollons would have had a great deal of interesting and important insights about how they would have analyzed Shirley Brice Heath's data—and vice versa—this never was done. Academics rarely analyze each others' data in ways that show how they would approach the same data from the perspectives of different disciplinary backgrounds and methodological tools.[1]

Many people working on DMAL have roots in or have been influenced by the NLS, the new literacies studies, situated cognition, or the NMLS. However, people working in the area have their own disciplinary affiliations over and beyond these spheres of affiliation or influence. Given the diverse backgrounds—in terms of movements and disciplines (e.g., educational technology, educational psychology, linguistics, ethnography, composition and rhetoric, media studies, communication, computer science, engineering, game design, and others)—of the people contributing to DMAL, what can or does give coherence to this emerging area? What are the commonalities (in thinking, language, assumptions, and methods) that can form the basis for collaboration?

Work in DMAL is, for the most part, at the stage of making plausibility arguments and offering limited proof-of-concept implementations. Nonetheless, these arguments and implementations now must begin to converge on a wider set of shared criteria of validity and warrants for claims that can serve both as a foundation for collaboration and eventually for more formal standards in the area. Doing so has the potential to shape the

1. Since I started the first draft of this book, Ron Scollon—one of the best academics of his generation—has passed away. He will be sorely missed. I dedicate this book to his memory.

speed at which the area grows by creating a kind of common ground against which ideas are developed.

Such a process of accelerating the growth of new focused areas of interdisciplinary study may be a necessity today. Global problems of climate change, poverty, over-population, energy crises, political instability, and cultural conflicts are fast reaching tipping points beyond which solutions will be severely limited or nonexistent (Friedman 2008). Today we must move faster than ever to engage in innovative problem solving around pressing issues—and education fit for an "at risk" global world in the twenty-first century is surely a pressing problem.

How, then, could we proceed in building this new area into something more integrated and coherent, especially in building collaboration? I suggest one way here, but there are others. We can take a clue from the literature on how other new areas have developed or how old areas have transformed themselves, especially the work of T. S. Kuhn (1970a, 1970b). However, I do not want to enter here into the massive, and now arcane, controversies over Kuhn's work and especially his term *paradigm* (e.g., Bird 2001; Fuller 2001; Kuhn 2000). Rather, my discussion in this book is inspired by a now-classic essay, making use of Kuhn in a specific way, by Eliot Mishler (1990) discussing what would constitute "validity" for yet another emerging area of study (an area that he called *inquiry research*).

Exemplars

What I take from Mishler's essay and my own reading of Kuhn is that for a new area, or a new approach in an established one, to gain traction and coherence it is necessary for certain examples of work—for example, analyses of data, applications of methods, theory building, or inferences from theories—to come to be seen as shared exemplars of what counts as "good work" or accepted work in the emerging area or approach. People may first come to share an appreciation for these exemplars as good work before they can articulate exactly why this is so. Indeed, such articulation by members of the emerging area or approach, as well as debate over what pieces of work constitute such exemplars, is one way in which shared theories, methods, language, models, and even values can emerge. What I was trying to do in *Sociolinguistics and Literacies* for the NLS was to point to what I and others thought were such exemplars. To the extent that others come to agree or propose other exemplars—as, indeed, many did in that case—the area emerges.

Such exemplars arise, of course, historically through the normal give and take of academic research working at the borders of different disciplines. What is important about such exemplars to an emerging area is that they focus debate in such a way that people, via that debate, come to articulate and share a common set of standards and values. These standards and values form, in turn, the foundation of the new area.

Exemplars normally arise naturally in the course of work in an emerging area, if they arise at all. What I want to propose here is that we could, in a sense, make a game (albeit a serious one) or market out of exemplars. Rather than waiting for the natural process to take its course, we could create "play exemplars" that we could use as tools for thought and debate. We could "bid" to have certain pieces of work accepted as exemplars and see if such bids—in comparison and contrast to others— began to energize debate, collaboration, and progress. One way such bidding could occur would be in a sort of "market" where contributors to DMAL listed exemplars they considered central to their vision of the area or an aspect of it. In turn, people could debate their different lists, clarifying how and why they viewed certain sorts of work or approaches potentially central for progress. Whether or not we actually created such a market, we could view the presentation of proposed exemplars as a new form of scholarship, one especially fit for developing new areas of inquiry.

Worked Examples

To make clear what I mean by *play exemplars*, consider another notion that is, in some ways, a polar opposite of the sorts of exemplars that have historically formed new areas, namely worked examples (Atkinson et al. 2000). Worked examples commonly are used to teach things like science and math. In a worked example, an "expert" takes a well-formed problem and publically displays for learners how that problem is approached, thought about, worked over, and solved. The worked example is meant to model for newcomers how an expert thinks, values, and acts in a given and well-established domain. In turn, newcomers can then try this and perhaps eventually find novel ways to solve problems in the domain as they "play" with various modeled approaches, because the model also can serve as a reference point from which to try variations.

Worked examples do not display just the individual thought of the expert. Rather, they exemplify the conventions of a discipline—the ways people in the area approach problems, how they recruit theories, and how they choose to continue when they face difficulties and dilemmas. Thus, worked examples are not associated with new emerging areas, areas still looking for exemplars that can serve as flags for new members of the emerging area to salute. They are associated with established areas.

So exemplars are things that eventually come to be seen as exemplary forms of work for a new area or a new approach to an old one. Worked examples are teaching devices used with students studying well-established areas. At first, then, these two things seem quite different. However, later in history, exemplars often come to be used as worked examples that serve as foundations for the area, not just for newcomers, but for full members (Kuhn 1970b, 187). At that point, once the new area is established, exemplars are both historically founding moments and, in the present, core examples of what counts as central and defining work in the area.

In a sense, exemplars, as they historically engendered the discussions and debates that eventually led to their acceptance as exemplars, served in the process as proposed worked examples for an area that did not yet exist. They were proposed worked examples (where the commentary on them was not just from their authors but from debates in the emerging area) not for students but for experts trying to build a new area in which there were as yet, in fact, no real experts. This is why, for instance, once an area is well established, teachers often use exemplary work in the area as worked examples for new students, displaying the thinking of the exemplar's author (thinking that often is discovered via historical research and which was, in actuality, a product of debate) as now "the discipline's" thinking.

What follows is a now-classic example of a proposed exemplar turning into fodder for common worked examples for students.

Thomas Kuhn (1970a) famously discussed how Galileo's ideas about motion introduced a new paradigm into physics. In people's everyday experience, an object set in motion always comes to a halt. Aristotle had argued that this was a fundamental property of nature: For motion to be sustained, an object must continue to be pushed.

Galileo proposed that we always observe objects coming to a halt simply because some friction is always present. He then proposed that without any friction to slow it down, an object in motion's inherent tendency is to maintain its speed without the application of any additional force. This bold idea about motion eventually reorganized physics and came to be seen as an exemplar that constituted modern physics as a discipline (and distinguished it from earlier physics). Today, of course, Galileo's ideas about force and motion are among the common material for worked examples in high school physics classes.

Worked Examples (In a New Sense) As a Way Forward

Scholars and practitioners in the emerging area of DMAL should propose from their own work or the work of others "play exemplars" (proposals about what an exemplar might look like). They would, in turn, work up these examples in just the way they might do for a worked example for students (although the "students" here are the scholars trying to build the emerging area). They would display publically their thinking about how and why they did what they did, and why it might serve as a guide for future work. This overt commentary on the example—the working of it—would initially be from the author of the proposed exemplar, but it would then engender public debate, discussion, and annotation from others, as well as response from the author. This public debate ultimately would become a sort of communal public working of the example.

This would be a new use for and sense of *worked examples*: attempts to imagine exemplars for a new area, and ways to create collaboration and debate around such proposed exemplars, in service of hastening actual exemplars and the growth of the area. Thus, scholars attempting to build the new area of

DMAL would display publically their ways of valuing and thinking about specific problems as suggestions about what might be an exemplar or an aspect of an exemplar for the area. They would do this to engender debate about what exemplars in the area might come to look like and, in turn, what shape the area might take. They would do this, too, to encourage collaboration that would lead to new worked examples—new proposals about what exemplars might look like—based on more shared criteria.

Thus, it would be like a game. Rather than wait—however long it takes—for history to tell us what the exemplars of the new area were (if, indeed, they ever did emerge), we should propose what they might look like (for a good start, see Sasha Barab's illuminating beginning worked examples using his *Quest Atlantis* work with commentary from others, which is available at http://inkido.indiana.edu/barab_we). The first proposals would, of course, be a bit too rooted in our own disciplines and backgrounds, but my hope is that discussion, debate, and collaboration would lead to further proposals that move toward shared theories, languages, and models of interventions. We would not need to wait, either, for full-blown exemplars to show up published in well-respected journals; transformative work in new areas or old ones often shows up at the margins of established areas, sometimes in forms rejected by established authorities, before it redefines what counts as a center.

Offering a worked example of a proposed exemplar might seem to be a big task if we take exemplars to be always "big" things, like whole theories, but they need not be big. An exemplar—and, too, the proposed play exemplars done as worked examples for others to work through themselves—could be small. It could be one application or aspect of a method or a theory, a bit of analysis, a way of combing a couple of ideas from different disciplines, one "move" in a proposed research project or learning intervention, and other things as well. The key point would be to propose and explicitly comment on some way of working, large or small, that might become a shared element—maybe after much debate and transformation—of the new area.

The point would be to exemplify publically how experts might talk about this element, if and when any experts were to arrive in this new area. The goal would not be to "win" (to have your work become an exemplar—history would take care of that for better or worse), but, in fact, to "lose," to see your proposed exemplar so worked over by the community that it would become fodder for collaboration that, in the end, would have no single author and would become not "you" but a new area of endeavor.

I propose, then, that we pretend to be experts in an area that as of yet has none. I propose that we treat each other as students working over problems as if they were well established even if they are not, so we actually know concretely what each other think and value, as a starting point, not as a finished point. Then we could imagine together new ways to think and work and, if successful, actually produce exemplars for a new area. These exemplars, if the area ever emerged, would, in turn, be used as worked examples for new students in the area. Maybe this game would work to accelerate the growth of a new area, but it would be a fine enough outcome if it merely served to create collaboration and the emergence of common ground through interaction and debate, and not just through the fiats of funders and established disciplinary journals.

The term *worked example* is heavily associated with science and math, but it need not be. I like the term because it stresses examples (cases, specifics) that are "worked," explicated in an overt way to make thinking public. Far from being germane only to science and math, this is similar to what artists and designers encounter in design workshops where they explicate, in an overt way, some of the creative processes that went into a piece of their work. The notion of a worked example, as I am extending the term here, is not unlike what goes on, as well, in some game-design "post mortems," as in the *Game Developer* or even what appears in some game designer's diaries and notebooks.

In the end, worked examples could become not just a way to move DMAL forward but also a new form of scholarship, one particularly fit for new areas of interdisciplinary, collaborative, thematically focused work (Barab, Dodge, and Gee, forthcoming). We could also imagine a Web site where a whole community contributes worked examples, comments on them, transforms and extends them, and links to other worked examples to form larger families of worked examples that would eventually start to both create and map the emerging area as it took shape.

A Worked-Example Example

The next chapter presents an example of a worked example. It is meant to exemplify a few points that may not be apparent from my previous discussion. These points are:

1. Although in an area like digital media and learning we can and should expect an effective use of multimedia in worked examples, the point is not media presentation but the presentation of argument, thinking, or approach.

2. I argued earlier that DMAL is not just about digital media but the wider workings of production and participation in popular culture. Thus, my example is from a card game that is also a set of video games, books, Web sites, television shows, and movies (an example of what Henry Jenkins (2006a) calls "convergent media").

3. A worked example does not have to be a big thing. It can also be about a small thing, or a small part of a big thing, as this example is.

4. This example comes out of my own disciplinary interests, which are not the disciplinary interests of most people in DMAL.

The point is: Do others see the claim I am making and my argument for it as a significant part of how they conceive the DMAL area or not, regardless of their own disciplinary affiliations? Such a judgment will reflect how they see DMAL taking shape in the future as a coherent area of study.

5. The point of the worked example is not to offer evidence—frankly we do not, as of yet, have much strong empirical evidence for many of the most interesting claims being made in DMAL. The point is to show the structure of the argument for which we need to collect evidence. It is impossible to match evidence and theory if we are not clear about the arguments underpinnings our theories.

6. One purpose of a worked example is to allow for comments from others, and even comments from the authors themselves (I have put in some comments of my own). They are also meant to inspire people to add their own related worked examples so a larger family of examples could emerge. In this example I argue for how Yu-Gi-Oh! recruits what I call "specialized language" and what this has to do with learning in and out of school. Others have argued that games like Yu-Gi-Oh! recruit and develop "systems thinking." Someone could add a worked example to mine along this line, extending the case. Someone else could add a worked example of how specialized language is recruited and developed in other games or other popular culture activities, or in Internet forums devoted to either. There would be many other ways to link to the example.

7. The worked example is meant to communicate to people outside my own discipline, so that one can see whether the ideas it contains resonate with the wider DMAL community or

some significant part of it. I may not have been completely successful here—it is a hard thing to do and one we all need to learn how to do better if we want to widen the impact of our work.

8. To avoid clutter, I have left out many of the references to research I could have included. This is meant to be merely an example to start off thinking on the nature and use of worked examples, so I wanted to stress the shape of the argument as much as I could.

9. In the end, one could see this worked example as a "bid" to see if a little bit of linguistics applied to DMAL would be seen as relevant to the area—something to build on and relate to—by those coming to DMAL from different disciplines. The larger enterprise of worked examples would have such cases from many different disciplines.

Worked Example: Yu-Gi-Oh!

Main Claim:

A. Today many popular culture activities involve complex language, more so than they did in the past.

> This claim and a related one that many popular culture activities involve complex thinking have been made recently by a variety of researchers from different areas and by more popular-press authors, as well. They are, I argue, one of the central arguments being made these days in the emerging field of digital media and learning.

B. Young people's engagement with such complex language is relevant to their success in school and society.

One Piece of Evidence for Main Claim (and the Subject of this Worked Example): Yu-Gi-Oh!

Relevant Version of Main Claim: Yu-Gi-Oh! involves complex language that is relevant to young people's success in school and society.

One serious problem at the outset: I treat learning in Yu-Gi-Oh! here as an individual and mental phenomenon, when (as I argue in my work on literacy and learning) it needs to be seen as social, cultural, and distributed. It would be important to develop relevant worked examples dealing with the social, cultural, distributed knowledge aspects of Yu-Gi-Oh! and link them to this one. On the other hand, my approach here is one way to gain surface validity for emerging work in digital media and learning from more well-established disciplines.

Comment: As a linguist I try to get at thinking through language—because different uses of language indicate different sorts of thinking—and so I here concentrate on language.

Clarifying Meaning/Significance of the Claim:

A. Yu-Gi-Oh! is a card game played, by people from about the age of 7 and up, face-to-face and via video games. It also is depicted in movies, television shows, and books; is described and discussed on many Web sites; and is a source of fan fiction.

Why This Is Interesting: Yu-Gi-Oh! is a case where young people engage in a set of activities that are spread across different media, digital and nondigital. In this respect it is an example of what Henry Jenkins calls "media convergence." Such media convergence is held to be typical of young people's popular culture today and is one aspect in which it is different and more complex than in the past. Further, Yu-Gi-Oh! is part of a global youth culture centered on anime, another new and arguably important phenomenon, especially in an increasingly global world.

My Agenda: I picked Yu-Gi-Oh! because I wanted my analysis to bear on the wider issues of (a) media convergence; (b) the mixture of the digital and the nondigital; and (c) global youth culture in a global world. I see Yu-Gi-Oh! as typical of the sort of out-of-school practices most central to the emerging area of digital media and learning

B. The term *complex* in *complex language* can have many different meanings. Here I am concerned with language that is "specialist" or "technical" in comparison to "vernacular" language ("everyday language" or "informal language," the style of language people use when they are communicating as "everyday people" and not in a role as a specialist or expert of any sort). Of course, in my analyses below I need to be specific about what makes specialist language—in this case, the language of Yu-Gi-Oh!—complex and why this sort of complexity is important for young people's school success and success in society after school.

Why This Is Interesting: The styles of language used in school connected to "content" areas like mathematics, science, and social studies—as well as the styles of language connected to academic disciplines—are called *academic language*.

"Academic language" is a big topic these days in educational linguistics. It has also been pervasive in current work on ESL and the education of immigrants and other nonnative speakers of English. I do not deal with this important issue here. A worked example, similar to the one here but dealing with ESL, would be important.

Academic language (composed of different styles for different domains) is one form of specialist or technical language. It has been claimed that the ability to read, write, speak, and comprehend academic language is one crucial key to school success. It is also arguable that being able to deal with specialist and technical forms of language is crucial for success in the public sphere and the work world young people will face after school. Our high-tech, science-driven, global culture creates such specialist and technical forms of language at a fast clip and demands facility with such forms of language.

My Agenda: I want to contrast learning a specialist style of language (like the one connected to Yu-Gi-Oh!) out of school with learning an academic language in school.

The contrast between learning outside school and learning in school has become a major motif in work in the emerging area of digital media and learning. Some controversy is beginning to grow over this contrast.

I want to do this in order to make claim two things:

(a) Although categories like poverty and race affect the learning of academic language in school, they do not, in the same way, affect the learning of a specialist language like that connected to Yu-Gi-Oh! out of school. Thus, such out-of-school learning is more equitable and may give us a guide to how to create such equity in school and out-of-school learning environments involving academic content.

> We are in desperate need of more research on how equity works in out-of-school learning. A worked example here, linked to this one, would be important.

(b) Learning a specialist style of language like that connected to Yu-Gi-Oh! will transfer to, or serve as "preparation for future learning" for, learning academic styles of language in school and dealing with specialist and technical styles of language after school in the public sphere and at work.

> The transfer question needs to be dealt with, and I have not done so. I am suggesting here that a "preparation for future learning" view of transfer would be a good way to go (Bransford and Schwartz 1999). A worked example here, linked to this one, would be important.

(i) Rationale for Why Yu-Gi-Oh! May Be Relevant to Success in School:

It is interesting that in outline form these two points are deeply embedded. But I must admit that one of my main goals in using Yu-Gi-Oh! has been to get these two points, common in the literacy literature, onto the table of the emerging area of digital media and learning.

(a) Early Vocabulary: Research on early literacy learning has indicated that a child's early vocabulary at age 5 is one of the most important predictors of school success after the child has learned to decode and thereafter for the rest of schooling. As a linguist I have argued that this finding is not about "everyday" words, but the words associated with books and schooling, that is, more formal and specialist vocabulary. Yu-Gi-Oh! involves a great deal of the sort of formal and specialist nonvernacular vocabulary associated with books, school, and academic content.

(b) Fourth-Grade Slump: Research over decades has indicated that many children who pass reading tests in the early grades cannot read well enough to learn school content by fourth grade, when the complex academic language connected to school content areas begins to become central to schooling. This leads to failure that stretches through middle school and high school. Yu-Gi-Oh! is a practice where young people have to read complex language in order to learn, but where the learning is lucid because it is associated with clear rules, actions, and images.

(ii) Rationale for Why Yu-Gi-Oh! May Be Relevant to Success after School:

I have done, in my work, a poor job of developing these rationales. Worked examples here, linked to this one, would be important.

(a) Technical and specialist styles of language are an important part of many modern professional and work practices.

(b) Civic participation as a global citizen requires mastery of complex vocabulary and other language forms associated with many complex issues.

Analysis and Methods

Figure 1

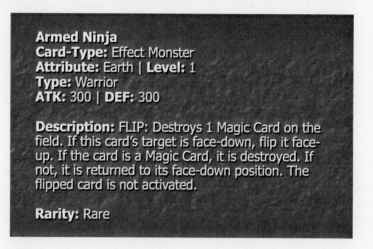

Armed Ninja
Card-Type: Effect Monster
Attribute: Earth | **Level:** 1
Type: Warrior
ATK: 300 | **DEF:** 300

Description: FLIP: Destroys 1 Magic Card on the field. If this card's target is face-down, flip it face-up. If the card is a Magic Card, it is destroyed. If not, it is returned to its face-down position. The flipped card is not activated.

Rarity: Rare

Figure 2

A. Complexity Analysis of the Card Above:

I use linguistics, psycholinguistics, and discourse analysis as my preferred methods of analysis. It would be important to see, in connected worked examples, how methods from different disciplines associated with the emerging area of digital media and learning would work here.

1. **Conditional Thinking:** This card involves three "if . . . then" conditional statements: (1) "If this card's target is face-down, flip it face-up"; (2) "If the card is a Magic card, it is destroyed"; (3) "If not, it is returned to its face-down position." Such statements involve logical "either-or" thinking.

2. **Deictics:** The deictic structure of this text is complex. (In linguistics, a deictic is any word whose referent is determined by the context in which it is said or written.) Readers must know that *this card* in "If this card's target is face down . . . " does not refer to "1 Magic Card on the field" in "Destroys 1 Magic Card on the field," but, rather, refers to the Armed Ninja card itself. *The card* in "If the card is a Magic Card" refers to the card that has been flipped up. *It* in "If not, it is returned . . . " also refers to the card that was flipped up (and is now to be flipped down). In the final sentence, the card that was flipped up (and now has been flipped down)—which has previously been referred to as *the card* and *it*—is now referred to as *the flipped card*. Readers must have a clear mental discourse model of the text in their head to render these references clear and fast.

3. **Macro Discourse Structure:** The first sentence ("Destroys 1 Magic Card on the field") gives the overall effect of the Armed Ninja card and is more like a heading for the whole passage than a direct part of the sentences that follow. The three following conditional statements describe how this overall affect is realized. The reader must realize that these three conditional statements are self contained (separate from the previous sentence) or the reader may take *this card* in "If this card's target is face down . . . " mistakenly to refer to "1 Magic Card in the field." The final statement ("The flipped card is not activated") is a clarification of the procedure described in the three conditional statements; it is otherwise unclear whether the flipped card should or should not be activated before it is flipped back down. In this sense, this final statement amounts to an excep-

tion clause: "Even though cards are normally activated when they are flipped up, this one is not." Readers must realize that this statement, although last, actually applies after "If this card's target is face-down, flip it face-up," because activation of cards normally happens when they are face-up.

What is my evidence for the claim that these features lead to complexity?

The evidence base here is years of research in psycholinguistics (language processing) that indicates that these sorts of linguistic features add greatly to the processing load when people are processing language.

Conditional clauses, especially one after the other, involve either-or thinking that is known to be difficult.

Complex deictics require the construction of a clear mental model for tracking reference, something that can be done only based on being able to integrate background knowledge and new knowledge (the text on the card) well.

Parsing the macro discourse structure of a text like this, where there are few overt indicators of the macro-structure, is also known to be difficult and to require the active recruitment of background knowledge and the integration of this knowledge with new knowledge (the text on the card). It also requires "genre knowledge" (knowledge of the genre of Yu-Gi-Oh! cards and related genres like Pokémon cards and Magic: The Gathering cards).

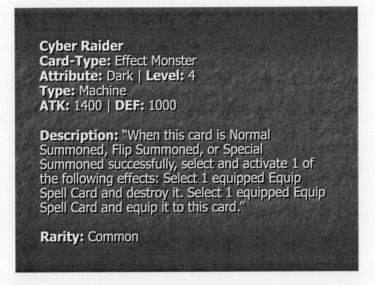

Cyber Raider
Card-Type: Effect Monster
Attribute: Dark | **Level:** 4
Type: Machine
ATK: 1400 | **DEF:** 1000

Description: "When this card is Normal Summoned, Flip Summoned, or Special Summoned successfully, select and activate 1 of the following effects: Select 1 equipped Equip Spell Card and destroy it. Select 1 equipped Equip Spell Card and equip it to this card."

Rarity: Common

Figure 3

Research indicates that such processing complexity in all these cases is more typical of written language than spoken language and more typical of academic language than vernacular language.

B. Complexity Analysis of the Card Above:

1. **Technical Terms:** *Normal summoned, flip summoned, special summoned, select, activate, equipped, equip spell card, destroy,* and *equipped equip spell card* are all technical terms in Yu-Gi-Oh!, equivalent to technical terms in any domain (such as, for example, law or biology).

2. **"Tier 2"**: Vocabulary: summon, select, activate, and effect are words that represent the typical vocabulary of written texts and the sorts of more-formal academic talk that are associated with school, academic disciplines, and the public sphere.

What is my evidence for the claim that these features lead to complexity?

Research on people learning new academic disciplines, even when they know another already, show that paying attention to technical terms—and being aware when a word is being used as a technical term and not being used with its more general non-technical meaning—is an important aspect of learning new disciplines and other technical domains of knowledge.

Research on vocabulary development distinguishes among three types of words (Beck, McKeown, and Kucan 2002): Tier 1 words are basic words that commonly appear in spoken language. Every native speaker knows these words and they do not need to be taught. Tier 2 words represent the more sophisticated vocabulary of written texts. Mature language users use these words regularly, but students, especially those from less advantaged homes, may encounter them less frequently as listeners. As a result, these words are unknown to many of our learners. Tier 3 words are technical terms that are limited to use in specific domains, such as medical and legal terms, or terms from academic disciplines. Tier 2 words are the words most often taught in school and the ones most crucial for success in school-based reading and listening. In the Yu-Gi-Oh! card above the Tier 2 words have technical uses related to their more general uses.

This example worked example is not meant to be typical. It is meant to show how one person from one specific background (i.e., linguistics) argues for a point of view he believes should be seen as important to the emerging area of DMAL. Others would construct their examples in a much more multimodal form, of course, but the point is that argument structure (or design decisions and reasons for them) and background assumptions should be made clear. If these are clear, then others can add their own viewpoints and compare and contrast other examples based on other backgrounds.

In the end, the purpose of my example worked example is to generate for each reader the following sorts of questions: Do you accept this set of claims as part of DMAL as you see it? If so, do you accept them as a significant or only trivial contribution to this area? What claims and accompanying arguments would you put forward as significant parts of DMAL as you see it?

If people do accept my example as a significant set of claims for DMAL, then we need to work together to get more evidence for these claims—or to falsify them, if that so happens—and to extend this example into a family of related examples (related in various different ways). If people do not accept my example as significant for DMAL, then, at least, we have learned something substantive about how they and I define the area and how we differ. Then we can move on to find examples whose significance for DMAL we all accept. If enough of us cannot find such examples, then no coherent area will emerge. If we can, we will be well on our way.

References

Alvermann, D. E., J. S. Moon, and M. C. Hagood. 1999. *Popular Culture in the Classroom: Teaching and Researching Critical Media Literacy.* Mahwah, NJ: Erlbaum.

Anderson, C. 2006. *The Long Tail: Why the Future of Business Is Selling Less of More.* New York: Hyperion.

Atkinson, R. K., S. J. Derry, A. Renkl, and D. W. Wortham. 2000. "Learning from Examples: Instructional Principles from the Worked Examples Research." *Review of Educational Research* 70, no. 2:181–214.

Barab, S. A., and C. Dede. 2007. "Games and Immersive Participatory Simulations for Science Education: An Emerging Type of Curricula." *Journal of Science Education and Technology* 16, no. 1:1–3.

Barab, S. A., T. Dodge, and J. P. Gee. Forthcoming. "The Worked Example: Invitational Scholarship in Service of an Emerging Field. *Educational Researcher.*

Barab, S. A., and W.-M. Roth. 2006. "Intentionally-Bound Systems and Curricular-Based Ecosystems: An Ecological Perspective on Knowing." *Educational Researcher* 35, no. 5:3–13.

Barsalou, L. W. 1999a. "Language Comprehension: Archival Memory or Preparation for Situated Action." *Discourse Processes* 28:61–80.

Barsalou, L. W. 1999b. "Perceptual Symbol Systems." *Behavioral and Brain Sciences* 22:577–660.

Bazerman, C. 1989. *Shaping Written Knowledge*. Madison: University of Wisconsin Press.

Beach, R. 2006. *Teachingmedialiteracy.com: A Web-Linked Guide to Resources and Activities*. New York: Teachers College Press.

Beck, I. L., M. G. McKeown, and L. Kucan. 2002. *Bringing Words to Life: Robust Vocabulary Instruction*. New York: Guildford Press.

Bennett, W. L., ed. 2007. *Civic Life Online: Learning How Digital Media Can Engage Youth* (John D. and Catherine T. MacArthur Foundation Series on Digital Media and Learning). Cambridge, MA: MIT Press.

Bird, A. 2001. *Thomas Kuhn*. Princeton, NJ: Princeton University Press.

Bizzell, P. 1992. *Academic Discourse and Critical Consciousness*. Pittsburgh, PA: University of Pittsburgh Press.

Black, R. W. 2008. *Adolescents and Online Fan Fiction*. New York: Peter Lang.

Brandt, D., and K. Clinton. 2002. "Limits of the Local: Expanding Perspectives on Literacy as a Social Practice." *Journal of Literacy Research* 34, no. 3:337–356

Bransford, J., A. L. Brown, and R. R. Cocking. 2000. *How People Learn: Brain, Mind, Experience, and School: Expanded Edition*. Washington, DC: National Academy Press.

Bransford, J. D., and D. Schwartz. 1999. "Rethinking Transfer: A Simple Proposal with Multiple Implications." In *Review of Research in Education*, vol. 24, eds. A. Iran-Nejad and P. D. Pearson, 61–100. Washington, DC: American Educational Research Association.

Brown, J. S., A. Collins, and P. Dugid. 1989. "Situated Cognition and the Culture of Learning." *Educational Researcher* 18, no. 1:32–42.

Brunner, C., and W. Tally. 1999. *The New Media Literacy Handbook: An Educator's Guide to Bringing New Media into the Classroom.* New York: Anchor.

Buckingham, D. 2003. *Media Education: Literacy, Learning and Contemporary Culture.* Cambridge, UK: Polity Press.

Buckingham, D., ed. 2007. *Youth, Identity, and Digital Media* (John D. and Catherine T. MacArthur Foundation Series on Digital Media and Learning). Cambridge, MA: MIT Press.

Cazden, C. 1985. "Research Currents: What Is Sharing Time For?" *Language Arts* 62, no. 2:182–188.

Cazden, C. 1988. *Classroom Discourse: The Language of Teaching and Learning.* Portsmouth, NH: Heinemann.

Churchland, P. S. 1986. *Neurophilosophy: Toward a Unified Science of the Mind/Brain.* Cambridge, MA: MIT Press.

Churchland, P. M. 1989. *A Neurocomputational Perspective: The Nature of Mind and the Structure of Science.* Cambridge, MA: MIT Press.

Churchland, P. S., and T. J. Sejnowski. 1992. *The Computational Brain.* Cambridge, MA: MIT Press.

Clark, A. 1989. *Microcognition: Philosophy, Cognitive Science, and Parallel Distributed Processing.* Cambridge, MA: MIT Press.

Clark, A. 1993. *Associative Engines: Connectionism, Concepts, and Representational Change.* Cambridge, UK: Cambridge University Press.

Clark, A. 1997. *Being There: Putting Brain, Body, and World Together Again.* Cambridge, MA: MIT Press.

Coiro, J., M. Knobel, C. Lankshear, and D. J. Le, eds. 2008. *Handbook of Research on New Literacies.* Philadelphia, PA: Lawrence Erlbaum.

Consalvo, M. 2007. *Cheating: Gaining Advantage in Videogames.* Cambridge, MA: MIT Press.

Cook-Gumperz, J., ed. 1986. *The Social Construction of Literacy*. Cambridge, UK: Cambridge University Press.

Damasio, A. R. 1994. *Descartes' Error: Emotion, Reason, and the Human Brain*. New York: Avon.

DiSessa, A. A. 2000. *Changing Minds: Computers, Learning, and Literacy*. Cambridge, MA: MIT Press.

Engeström, Y. 1987. *Learning by Expanding: An Activity Theoretical Approach to Developmental Research*. Helsinki: Orienta Konsultit.

Everett, A., ed. 2007. *Learning Race and Ethnicity: Youth and Digital Media* (John D. and Catherine T. MacArthur Foundation Series on Digital Media and Learning). Cambridge, MA: MIT Press.

Friedman, T. L. 2008. *Hot, Flat, and Crowded: Why We Need a Green Revolution—and How It Can Renew America*. New York: Farrar, Straus, & Giroux.

Fuller, S. 2001. *Thomas Kuhn: A Philosophical History of Our Times*. Chicago: University of Chicago Press.

Gee, J. P. 1985. "The Narrativization of Experience in the Oral Style." *Journal of Education*,167, no. 1:9–35.

Gee, J. P. 1987. "What Is Literacy?" *Teaching and Learning* 2, no. 1:3–11.

Gee, J. P. 1990. *Social Linguistics and Literacies: Ideology in Discourses*. London: Taylor & Francis. 2nd ed. 1996; 3rd ed. 2007.

Gee, J. P. 1992. *The Social Mind: Language, Ideology, and Social Practice*. New York: Bergin & Garvey.

Gee, J. P. 2000. "The New Literacy Studies: From 'Socially Situated' to the Work of the Social." In *Situated Literacies: Reading and Writing in Context*, eds. D. Barton, M. Hamilton, and R. Ivanic, 180–196. London: Routledge.

Gee, J. P. 2003. *What Video Games Have to Teach Us about Learning and Literacy*. New York: Palgrave/Macmillan. 2nd ed. 2007.

Gee, J. P. 2004. *Situated Language and Learning: A Critique of Traditional Schooling.* London: Routledge.

Gee, J. P. 2005. *Why Video Games Are Good for Your Soul: Pleasure and Learning.* Melbourne: Common Ground.

Gee, J. P. 2007. *Good Video Games and Good Learning: Collected Essays on Video Games, Learning, and Literacy.* New York: Peter Lang.

Gee, J. P. 2008. *Getting Over the Slump: Innovation Strategies to Promote Children's Learning.* New York: The Joan Ganz Cooney Center at Sesame Workshop.

Gell-Mann, M. 1994. *The Quark and the Jaguar.* New York: Freeman & Co.

Glenberg, A. M. 1997. "What Is Memory For." *Behavioral and Brain Sciences* 20:1–55.

Goody, J. 1977. *The Domestication of the Savage Mind.* Cambridge, UK: Cambridge University Press.

Goody, J., and I. P. Watt. 1963. "The Consequences of Literacy." *Comparative Studies in History and Society* 5:304–345.

Graff, H. J. 1979. *The Literacy Myth: Literacy and Social Structure in the Nineteenth-Century City.* New York: Academic Press.

Havelock, E. 1976. *Preface to Plato.* Cambridge, MA: Harvard University Press.

Hawkins, J. 2005. *On Intelligence.* New York: Henry Holt.

Heath, S. B. 1983. *Ways with Words: Language, Life, and Work in Communities and Classrooms.* Cambridge, UK: Cambridge University Press.

Hobbs, R. 1997. "Expanding the Concept of Literacy." In *Media Literacy in the Information Age: Current Perspectives,* ed. R. Kuby, 163–183. New Brunswick, NJ: Transaction Publisher.

Hobbs, R. 2007. *Reading the Media: Media Literacy in High School English.* New York: Teachers College Press.

Holland, J. H. 1998. *Emergence: From Chaos to Order*. Reading, MA: Addison-Wesley.

Hull, G. A., and K. Schultz. 2001. *School's Out: Bridging Out-of-School Literacies with Classroom Practice*. New York: Teachers College Press.

Hutchins, E. 1995. *Cognition in the Wild*. Cambridge, MA: MIT Press.

Ito, M., H. A. Horst, M. Bittanti, d. boyd, B. Herr-Stephenson, P. G. Lange, C. J. Pascoe, and L. Robinson. 2010. *Living and Learning with New Media: Summary of Findings from the Digital Youth Project* (The John D. and Catherine T. MacArthur Foundation Reports on Digital Media and Learning). Cambridge, MA: MIT Press.

Jenkins, H. 1992. *Textual Poachers: Television Fans and Participatory Culture*. New York: Routledge.

Jenkins, H. 2006a. *Convergence Culture: Where Old and New Media Collide*. New York: New York University Press.

Jenkins, H. 2006b. *Fans, Bloggers, and Gamers: Media Consumers in a Digital Age*. New York: New York University Press.

Jenkins, H., with R. Purushotma, M. Weigel, K. Clinton, and A. J. Robison. 2009. *Confronting the Challenges of Participatory Culture: Media Education for the 21st Century* (The John D. and Catherine T. MacArthur Foundation Reports on Digital Media and Learning). Cambridge, MA: MIT Press.

Johnson, S. 2005. *Everything Bad Is Good for You: How Today's Popular Culture Is Actually Making Us Smarter*. New York: Riverhead.

Kirschner, P. A., K. Sweller, and R. E. Clark. 2006. "Why Minimal Guidance During Instruction Does Not Work: An Analysis of the Failure of Constructivist, Discovery, Problem-Based, Experiential, and Inquiry-Based Teaching." *Educational Psychologist* 41:75–86.

Kist W. 2004. *New Literacies in Action: Teaching and Learning in Multiple Media*. New York: Teachers College Press.

Knobel, M., and C. Lankshear, eds. 2007. *A New Literacies Sampler*. New York: Peter Lang.

Kolodner, J. L. 1993. *Case-Based Reasoning*. San Mateo, CA: Morgan Kaufmann Publishers.

Kolodner, J. L. 2006. "Case-Based Reasoning." In *The Cambridge Handbook of the Learning Sciences*, ed. R. K. Sawyer, 225–242. Cambridge, UK: Cambridge University Press.

Kress, G. 2003. *Literacy in the New Media Age*. London: Routledge.

Kuhn, T. S. 1970a. *The Structure of Scientific Revolutions*. 2nd ed., enlarged. Chicago, IL: University of Chicago Press

Kuhn, T. S. 1970b. "Reflections on My Critics." In *Criticism and the Growth of Knowledge*, eds. I. Lakatos and A. Musgrave, 231–278. London: Cambridge University Press.

Kuhn, T. S. 2000. *The Road since Structure: Philosophical Essays, 1970–1993*. Chicago, IL: University of Chicago Press.

Lankshear, C. 1997. *Changing Literacies*. Berkshire, UK: Open University Press.

Lankshear, C., and M. Knobel. 2006. *New Literacies*. 2nd ed. Berkshire, UK: Open University Press.

Latour, B. 2004. *Politics of Nature: How to Bring the Sciences into Democracy*. Cambridge, MA: Harvard University Press.

Latour, B. 2005. *Reassembling the Social: An Introduction to Actor-Network-Theory*. Oxford: Oxford University Press.

Lave, J. 1996. "Teaching, As Learning, In Practice." *Mind, Culture, and Activity* 3:149–164.

Lave, J., and E. Wenger. 1991. *Situated Learning: Legitimate Peripheral Participation*. New York: Cambridge University Press.

Leadbeater, C., and P. Miller. 2004. *The Pro-Am Revolution: How Enthusiasts Are Changing Our Society and Economy*. London: Demos.

Lenhardt, A., and M. Madden. 2005. *Teen Content Creators and Consumers*. Washington, DC: Pew Internet & American Life Project. Available online at http://www.pewInternet.org/PPF/r/166/report_display.asp.

Lewin, R. 1992. *Complexity: Life at the Edge of Chaos*. New York: MacMillan.

McPherson, T., ed. 2007. *Digital Youth, Innovation, and the Unexpected* (John D. and Catherine T. MacArthur Foundation Series on Digital Media and Learning). Cambridge, MA: MIT Press.

Metzger, M. J., and A. J. Flanagin, eds. 2007. *Digital Media, Youth, and Credibility* (John D. and Catherine T. MacArthur Foundation Series on Digital Media and Learning). Cambridge, MA: MIT Press.

Michaels, S. 1981. "'Sharing Time': Children's Narrative Styles and Differential Access to Literacy." *Language in Society* 10, no. 4:423–442.

Mishler, E. G. 1990. "Validation in Inquiry-Guided Research: The Role of Exemplars in Narrative Studies." *Harvard Educational Review* 60, no. 4: 415–442.

Newell, A., and H. A. Simon. 1972. *Human Problem Solving*. Englewood Cliffs, NJ: Prentice-Hall.

New London Group. 1996. "A Pedagogy of Multiliteracies: Designing Social Futures." *Harvard Education Review* 66, no. 1:60–92.

Olson, D. R. 1977. "From Utterance to Text: The Bias of Language in Speech and Writing." *Harvard Education Review* 47:257–8.

Ong, W. J. 1982. *Orality and Literacy: The Technologizing of the Word*. London: Methuen.

Pahl, K., and J. Rowsel. 2005. *Literacy and Education: Understanding the New Literacy Studies in the Classroom*. London: Paul Chapman.

Pahl, K., and J. Rowsel, eds. 2006. *Travel Notes from the New Literacy Studies: Instances of Practice*. Clevedon, UK: Multilingual Matters.

Prinsloo, M., and B. Mignonne, eds. 1996. *The Social Uses of Literacy: Theory and Practice in Contemporary South Africa*. Philadelphia: John Benjamins.

Rumelhart, D. E., J. L. McClelland, and the PDP Research Group. 1986. *Parallel Distributed Processing: Explorations in the Microstructure of Cognition: Vol. 1 Foundations*. Cambridge, MA: MIT Press.

Salen, K, ed. 2007a. *The Ecology of Games: Connecting Youth, Games, and Learning* (John D. and Catherine T. MacArthur Foundation Series on Digital Media and Learning). Cambridge, MA: MIT Press.

Salen, K. 2007b. "Gaming Literacies: What Kids Learn through Design." *Journal of Educational Multimedia and Hypermedia* 16, no. 3:301–322.

Salen, K., and E. Zimmerman 2003. *Rules of Play: Game Design Fundamentals*. Cambridge, MA: MIT Press.

Sawyer, R. K., ed. 2006. *The Cambridge Handbook of the Learning Sciences*. Cambridge, UK: Cambridge University Press.

Scollon, R., and S. B. K. Scollon. 1981. *Narrative, Literacy, and Face in Interethnic Communication*. Norwood, NJ: Ablex.

Scribner, S., and Cole, M. 1981. *The Psychology of Literacy*. Cambridge, MA: Harvard University Press.

Shaffer, D. W. 2004. "Pedagogical Praxis: The Professions As Models for Post-industrial Education." *Teachers College Record* 10:1401–1421.

Shaffer, D. W. 2005. "Epistemic Games." *Innovate* 1, no. 6. Available online at http://www.innovateonline.info/index.php?view=article&id=81.

Shaffer, D. W. 2007. *How Computer Games Help Children Learn*. New York: Palgrave/Macmillan.

Shaffer, D. W., K. Squire, R. Halverson, and J. P. Gee. 2005. "Video Games and the Future of Learning." *Phi Delta Kappan* 87, no. 2:104–111.

Shirky, C. 2008. *Here Comes Everybody: The Power of Organizing without Organizations.* New York: Penguin.

Steinkuehler, C. A. 2006. "Massively Multiplayer Online Videogaming As Participation in a Discourse." *Mind, Culture, & Activity* 13, no. 1:38–52.

Steinkuehler, C. A. 2008a. "Cognition and literacy in Massively Multiplayer Online Games." In *Handbook of Research on New Literacies,* eds. J. Coiro, M. Knobel, C. Lankshear, and D. Leu, 611–634. Mahwah, NJ: Erlbaum.

Steinkuehler, C. 2008b. "Massively Multiplayer Online Games As an Educational Technology: An Outline for Research." *Educational Technology* 48, no. 1:10–21.

Street, B. 1984. *Literacy in Theory and Practice.* Cambridge, UK: Cambridge University Press.

Street, B. 1993. "Introduction: The New Literacy Studies." In *Cross-Cultural Approaches to Literacy,* ed. B. Street, 1–21. New York: Cambridge University Press.

Street, B. 1995. *Social Literacies: Critical Approaches to Literacy in Development, Ethnography, and Education.* London: Longman.

Street, B. 1997. "The Implications of the 'New Literacy Studies' for Literacy Education." *English in Education* 31, no. 3:45–59.

Street, B. 2005. "At Last: Recent Applications of New Literacy Studies in Educational Contexts." *Research in the Teaching of English* 39, no. 4:417–423.

Squire, K. D. 2006. "From Content to Context: Video Games As Designed Experience." *Educational Researcher* 35, no. 8:19–29.

Squire, K. 2007. "Games, Learning, and Society: Building a Field." *Educational Technology* 4, no. 5:51–54.

Squire, K., and H. Jenkins. 2004. "Harnessing the Power of Games in Education." *Insight* 3, no. 1:5–33.

Waldrop, M. M. 1992. *Complexity: The Emerging Science at the Edge of Chaos*. New York: Simon and Schuster.

Warschauer, M. 1998. *Electronic Literacies: Language, Culture, and Power in Online Education*. Mahwah, NJ: Erlbaum.

Wenger, E. 1998. *Communities of Practice: Learning, Meaning, and Identity*. Cambridge, UK: Cambridge University Press.

Wertsch, J. V. 1985. *Vygotsky and the Social Formation of Mind*. Cambridge, MA: Harvard University Press.

Wilensky, U., and K. Reisman. 2006. "Thinking like a Wolf, a Sheep, or a Firefly: Learning Biology through Constructing and Testing Computational Theories—An Embodied Modeling Approach." *Cognition & Instruction* 24, no. 2:171–209.

Zimmerman, E. 2007. "Game Design As a Model of Literacy for the 21st Century." *Harvard Interactive Media Review* 1, no. 1:30–35.